The Costume

5000 Years of Fashion History

Timeline

CLAUDIA MÜLLER

THAMES AND HUDSON

INDIA JAPAN 20TH CENTURY INDONESIA MALAYSIA

EUROPE EUROPE

GUATEMALA TRINIDAD MOROCCO SENEGAMBIA NIGER

ASIA 1 Working man: kurta, lungi. **2** Salwar kameez. **3** Noblewoman: traditional dress. **4** Peasant: tunic, skirt. **5** Wicker hat. **6** Ceremonial dress, long scarf over one shoulder. **7** Village headman: official dress, Western-style jacket, long sarong. **8** Townswoman: long close-fitting dress, modern accessories. **9, 10** Peasants: shirts, trousers, 'coolie' hats.

EUROPE 1 Loose-fitting slacks with turn-ups. **2** Belted coat, beret. **3** Calf-length evening dress, shoes with ankle-straps. **4** Single-breasted suit, tie. **5** Pullover, mid-length skirt. **6** Mini-dress. **7** Mini-dress, thigh-boots. **8** Denim suit, flared trousers. **9** Evening wear, long waisted jacket, flared trousers. **10** Suede jacket and trousers. **11** Punk: studded leather jacket, jeans.

AMERICA AND AFRICA 1 Modern shirt, traditional trousers and waist-sash. **2** Typical head-dress, printed material knotted across one shoulder. **3** Mother and child. **4, 5** Pair of dancers. **6** Drummer: jellaba. **7** Dress designs celebrating union of Senegal and The Gambia. **8** Batik robe. **9** Traditional dress, modern accessories. **10** Westernized dress.

CHINA

20TH CENTURY

INDIA

EUROPE

EUROPE

PERU

U.S.A.

MEXICO

ASIA 1, 2 Mandarins: ceremonial dress, distinguishing hats. **3** Guard: long robe, conical hat. **4** Guard: short jacket, trousers, pigtail. **5** Lower-class woman and baby: slit tunic, long gown. **6** Noblewoman: bound feet. **7** Rajah: gem-encrusted state dress, pearls, decorations. **8** Noblewoman: sari. **9** Musician: waistcoat, pajama. **10** Noble: close-fitting coat. **11** Doctor.

EUROPE 1, 2 Bathing costumes. **3** Informal wear, overcoat, bowler hat. **4** Town dress, long jacket, ostrich-feather hat. **5** Boy dressed for motoring. **6** Long day dress, hat with feathers. **7** Evening wear, pleated tunic, skirt with train. **8** Printed silk coat, cloche hat, fox stole. **9** Tweed suit. **10** Knickerbocker suit, peaked cap. **11** Summer wear, short skirt, shingled hair. **12** Sun-suit.

AMERICA 1, 2 Quechua couple: traditional dress. **3** Cowboy: stetson, leather chaps. **4** Hunter: skin jacket and boots. **5** Apache woman: modern shirt, traditional accessories. **6** Apache woman, papoose on back. **7, 8** Middle-class Black couple. **9** Embroidered dress, lace trimmings.

The Costume

5000 Years of Fashion History

Timeline

This book sets out to show how people have dressed over the centuries throughout the world. It is not an exhaustive academic work, but rather a wide-ranging overview of dress and ornament, from the fig leaf to haute couture, for the general reader, the designer or the student.

Cloth and leather are perishable materials and little has survived of dress from before the 18th century. Many of the costumes illustrated here have been drawn from works of art (paintings, sculptures, tapestries, etc.) and archaeological finds of diverse periods and provenances. Only for recent times have we been able to use existing models and photographs. Chronology is also approximate: fashion does not progress in a straight line and works of art do not always reflect objective reality. Nowadays we know enough about ancient textiles and dyes to say with some degree of accuracy what they were like in any given period, and this has helped us immensely in the reconstructions in this book. People probably started wearing clothes for climatic reasons – for shelter from heat or cold – since, unlike other animals, humans do not have fur or a significant amount of body hair. However, in time, this practical reason became a secondary factor and people in every society were soon dressing according to precise rules by which ornament and dress came chiefly to express social status. People started to conceal in order to reveal.

Not everyone was entitled to wear the same costume: think of a king or a priest (of any cult) or a soldier or dignitary, all of whom are immediately recognizable by their dress which they wear only by virtue of their status. Traditional symbolic or emblematic features tend to be accentuations of functional elements, the purpose being to stress the ideal personality of the religious or civil official. For example, the mantle is a symbol of royal investiture, the crown of majesty or the privileged relationship with the divine. Ermine, the colour purple, and accessories like the sceptre, the pastoral staff or certain precious stones all have symbolic value.

Not only what to wear, but also how much to wear, has always been an important point, affected by social standing, prejudice, magic or modesty, as the case may be. The concept of modesty varies enormously from one civilization to another and each period in history has followed its own rules. Women in Minoan Crete went bare-breasted, and countless generations of African women have never clothed their upper bodies. Among Moslem women some still wear the *chador*, a garment which conceals the entire head and body, while others cover their faces with a veil. For some cultures dress means simply a waist-band or a body decoration.

Within the confines of culture and function there has always been room for novelty and difference, perhaps to express the inborn human need to amuse and be amused, to please and be pleased, to impress or attract members of the opposite sex, or even to emphasize or alter one's personality.

Pursuing an abstract ideal of beauty, people have seldom taken into account the limits and restrictions imposed by the human body. Corsets have been used throughout history. They were worn by women and men alike in Knossos. To restrict the body even further within an ideal geometrical shape, in 16th-century Spain women's skirts were rigidly supported by iron stays (the farthingale) and took the form of a truncated cone.

In pursuit of the same ideal of beauty, people have even tried to reshape their anatomy. The Moche Indians of South America deformed the skulls of their children by binding them between wooden boards; in pre-revolutionary China, rich women's feet were tightly bound from childhood on to keep them tiny; other peoples in Africa, Oceania and America have decorated themselves by scarring the body or tattooing it with designs. Body painting, far from being practised solely for decoration or fun, expresses precise social meanings in its patterns. As a substitute for clothing, the styles and patterns express the society's hierarchy of rules, filling the gap between nature and culture and stressing the difference between the 'simple' animal and the more 'sophisticated' human being.

The innumerable transformations which dress has undergone through the ages can be summarized into six basic types:
(1) The wrapped and draped dress of ancient Egypt, Greece, Rome and India
(2) The fitted dress, as in ancient Northern Europe, medieval Europe, and Anatolia and Arabia
(3) The stitched, fitted dress, as in Persia, Turkmenistan and the Balkans
(4) The stitched open dress, or caftan, as in Central Asia, Russia and Europe
(5) The long, full-cut robe with broad sleeves of China, Japan, Mongolia and Siberia
(6) The tight-fitting dress, as in the Arctic and Central Asia.

These basic types had, and indeed still have, many variations. Dress has always been affected by cultural, political and economic conditions.

The ancient Mediterranean civilizations wore the draped dress for many centuries, up until the fall of the Roman Empire. The spread of Christianity and the expansion of the 'barbarian' world brought about enormous changes in dress. Breeches and furs, as well as the stitched, fitted dress, arrived in the West from Asia.

With the rise of the middle classes, the aesthetic value of dress gained in importance and both the word and the notion of 'elegance' entered the common vocabulary.

Social change as well as political events, such as marriages between rulers of different peoples, international trade and travel, scientific discoveries, personal taste, and so on, have all affected the way people dress. Missionaries brought the silkworm to Byzantium from Asia; the British brought cotton muslin from India; the invention of the spinning machine led to the widespread use of voluminous women's undergarments; under Louis XIV Madame de Montespan imposed her taste for gold *passementerie*, lace and ribbons; the French Revolution brought about some drastic changes in dress, which have only ever been equalled by the changes caused by World War II. Recent technological innovation has produced artificial fibres, chemical dyes and ready-to-wear, fitted clothing. Now, for the first time, we can speak of a true revolution in dress and ornament for millions of people throughout the world. Fashion changes rapidly in our society.

Even so, there are still some underlying styles and trends which persist practically unchanged; after more than one hundred and fifty years, men's 'smart' dress – the suit, complete with tie – is still in use all over the world.

ASIA

EUROPE

AFRICA AND AMERICA

19TH CENTURY

PERSIA   CHINA

EUROPE

U.S.A.   U.S.A.

ASIA 1 Noble child. **2** Prince: long colourful tunic, cylindrical cap. **3** Noblewoman: long baggy trousers. **4** Veiled woman. **5** Noble warrior. **6** Mullah: turban, holy book. **7** Prince. **8** King: silk brocade, pearls, precious stones. **9** Commander of the imperial guard: distinguishing cross-belts. **10** Cavalry general.

EUROPE 1 Morning dress, lace bonnet with bows. **2** Fur-edged double coat, muff, small hat with veil at back. **3** Walking costume, flared coat over full skirt. **4** Low-cut gown. **5** Crinoline gown with stomacher. **6** Sailor suit. **7** High-necked gown, balloon sleeves, feather hat. **8** Visiting dress with bustle. **9** Check sporting wear, bowler hat. **10, 11** Couple in travelling dress.

AMERICA 1 Warrior: painted body, skin trousers. **2** Chief with peace-pipe. **3** Low-necked crinoline gown, half-sleeves. **4** Town wear, bonnet tied under chin. **5, 6** Unionist officer and soldier in uniform. **7** Confederate officer in uniform. **8** Lower-class woman: bonnet, shawl, apron. **9** Boy dressed as soldier.

RUSSIA   19TH CENTURY   RUSSIA   PERSIA

EUROPE   EUROPE

MEXICO   ARGENTINA PERU CHILE CANADA   U.S.A.

ASIA 1, 2 Gentlewomen: fur hat, embroidered skins and furs. **3** Conical hat with broad curled brim. **4** Hunter (Mongolia). **5** Young girl. **6** Townswoman: walking dress (Kazan). **7, 8, 9** Samoyed family: furs (Siberia). **10** Servant: printed shawl around waist. **11** Servant. **12** Dancer: close-fitting bodice, hoop skirt.

EUROPE 1 Empire gown. **2** Chemise gown, poke bonnet. **3** Walking dress with flounces, bonnet on back of head. **4** Walking dress, puffed sleeves with epaulettes. **5** Tail-coat buttoned from collar to waist. **6** Coat, trousers, stovepipe hat. **7** Girl's dress with double collar. **8** Boy's shirt tied at the waist, trousers. **9** Riding habit. **10** Travelling dress, top hat, coat, cape.

AMERICA 1 Low-cut gown, comb in hair. **2** Gown raised to show underskirt. **3** Striped tunic, lace-trimmed knee-breeches. **4** Gaucho: poncho, sandals with spurs. **5** Woman's tall hat. **6** Poncho, boots. **7** Decorated boot. **8** Chief's head-dress. **9** Shaman's painted gourd (Tlingit). **10** Chief: ceremonial dress, blanket over shoulders (Tlingit). **11** Embroidered skin clothing. **12** Sorcerer.

CENTRAL EUROPE   HUNGARY

ALGERIA   EGYPT   EGYPT

ASIA 1 Dignitary: sheepskin skirt. **2** Soldier: helmet, studded leather stole. **3** Dignitary. **4, 5** Gold helmet, queen's head-dress and jewelry (Ur). **6** Official: cloak knotted on one shoulder. **7** Noble: tunic open at one side. **8** Archer: draped robe, fringe and geometric designs. **9** Multi-coloured fabric with various designs wrapped around the body. **10, 11** Pharaoh's bodyguards.

EUROPE 1 Hunter: furs and trousers made of skins (Palaeolithic). **2** Hunter: skins wrapped around hips. **3** Shaman: furs with horns. **4** Burin (Lepenski Vir). **5** Dagger (Lepenski Vir). **6** Stone engraved with human face. **7** Razor (Lepenski Vir). **8** Garments of stitched skins. **9** Hunter: trousers of skin. **10** Bust of a goddess (Szentes).

AFRICA 1, 2 Hunters: painted bodies (Tassili). **3** Standard-bearer: draped loincloth (shenti). **4** Pharaoh: crown, sceptre, false beard. **5** Pharaoh: official dress with double crown, false beard, collar, stylized loincloth with gems, staff. **6** Queen: crown of vulture feathers. **7** Princess. **8** Slave. **9** Priest: leopardskin to indicate status.

BALKANS

CENTRAL EUROPE

SOUTHERN EUROPE

EGYPT

EGYPT

ASIA 1, 2 Ephod over sleeved robe with waist-sash.
3, 4 Notables: fringed cloaks. **5** Seven-branched candle-
stick. **6** Clay vase. **7** Priest: ephod, turban. **8** Lower-class
woman: conical head-dress. **9** Caftan with tassels, clasp
fastening. **10** Waistcoat, open at the breast, full trousers
(Dorak). **11** Loincloth, cylindrical head-dress with veil
(Dorak). **12** Loincloth, conical head-dress (Dorak).

EUROPE 1 Female figurine (Cucute). **2** Seated woman
(Vinca). **3** Woven garment, fastened at shoulder and
waist. **4** Draped garment. **5** Short tunic, hat. **6** Cloak
over shoulders and head. **7, 8** Bone comb and necklace
(Balkans). **9** Woven fabric (Switzerland). **10** Lyre-player
(Cyclades). **11** Plaque with owl design (Milares, Portugal).
12 Gold plaque, perhaps a belt-end (Sicily).

AFRICA 1 Princess: collar and jewelled wig. **2** Staff of
office. **3** Flabellum of the Pharaoh. **4, 11** Soldiers: cloth
head-dress. **5** Slave: long tunic. **6** Slave: short tunic with
straps, exposing the breasts. **7** Slave: long tunic with
straps. **8** Mirror. **9** Sandals. **10** Slave: loincloth. **12** Slave:
draped loincloth (shenti).

18TH CENTURY VIETNAM THAILAND BURMA SRI LANKA

FRANCE FRANCE

U.S.A. OCEANIA AND AUSTRALIA

ASIA 1 Noble: conical cap bent forward, costly kimono. **2** Noblewoman. **3** Official: distinguishing sash. **4** Noble: tall conical head-dress, baggy trousers. **5** Layered skirt, open in front. **6** Seaman: short jacket, long gown, trousers. **7** Prince: cushion-shaped head-dress, frilled trousers. **8** Monk. **9** Village headman: crown, distinguishing sash. **10** Temple dancer.

EUROPE 1 Pleated bonnet. **2** Walking dress, skirt over frame. **3** Fur-bordered cloak, muff. **4** Gown with 'sails' over frame. **5** Walking dress, tricorn hat, fitted coat. **6** Cloak draped behind. **7** Coat with lapel-buttons. **8** Tail-coat, tall hat with curled brim. **9** Boy's striped suit. **10** High-waisted gown over frame. **11** Bicorn hat, long coat with tiered shoulder-cape.

AMERICA AND OCEANIA 1, 2 Quakers. **3** Coat with broad cuffs, neck-cloth. **4** Slave: trousers, straw hat. **5** Wealthy bourgeoise: loose gown with train. **6** Slave: kerchief crossed over the breast. **7** Warrior: ceremonial costume of plant fibres (New Ireland). **8** Warrior: fibre skirt (New Ireland). **9** Aborigine: painted body (Australia). **10** Warrior: painted and tattooed body (Marquesas).

GREAT BRITAIN

GERMANY

Jews from Algeria   *Moors from Algeria*   *and Tunisia*   U.S.A.

ASIA 1 Samurai: swords in obi, kimono with emblems.
2 Servant. **3** Official. **4** Lady of the court: elaborate hair-style, shaven-headed baby. **5** Prince: full robes, apron sash, fan, distinguishing hair-style. **6** Servant. **7** Geisha. **8, 9** Ladies of the court.

EUROPE 1 Gentleman: long curled wig, open coat over waistcoat, neck-cloth, high-heeled ankle-boots. **2** Long floral waistcoat. **3** Gentleman: tricorn hat, high buttoned boots with spurs. **4, 5** Middle-class couple: country dress, straw hat. **6** Noblewoman: day dress, wide skirt over frame. **7** Gentlewoman: shoulder-cape, bonnet. **8, 9** Noble couple: hunting attire.

AFRICA AND AMERICA 1, 2 Embroidered deerskin purse and moccasin. **3** Short jacket over wide knee-breeches. **4, 5** Children of wealthy merchant class dressed like adults. **6** Waistcoat over jacket, turban with tassel. **7** Veiled woman. **8** Prince: short waistcoat, wide robe. **9, 10** Children of lower class. **11** Fur-trader dressed in skins.

2000 BC

ASSYRIA BABYLON BABYLON

CRETE AND MYCENAE   CRETE AND MYCENAE

EGYPT   EGYPT

ASIA 1 Polychrome vase (Susa). **2** Female figurine: flounced garment (Bactria). **3** Slave. **4** Slave carrying parasol, insignia of the king. **5** Official. **6, 7** High officials: distinguishing fringed sashes. **8** Scribe. **9** Shield. **10** Sickle. **11** Fly-whisk. **12, 13** Sandals. **14, 15** Head-dresses. **16** Clay vase.

EUROPE 1 Noble: short tunic. **2** Soldier. **3** Huntress: layered, multi-coloured embroidered skirt. **4** King: tasselled tunic, shorts and boots. **5** Soldier: short trousers with geometric border. **6** Soldier: helmet, tunic, greaves. **7** Boxer: double apron, longer at the back, with metal lining.

AFRICA 1 Pharaoh's slave. **2** Official. **3** Pharaoh: cloth head-dress with cobra emblem. **4** Pharaoh: head-dress with cobra emblem, wide collar, stylized loincloth. **5** Queen: crown of vulture feathers. **6** Funerary mask of Tutankhamun. **7** Pectoral. **8** Cup. **9** Royal insignia. **10** Mummy in sarcophagus. **11, 12** Queen's slaves. **13** Menial slave: tunic with straps, exposing the breasts.

CRETE AND MYCENAE CRETE AND MYCENAE

EGYPT EGYPT

ASIA 1 King: ceremonial dress, high head-dress, cloak, fringed tunic. **2** King dressed as high priest. **3** Priest's assistant. **4** Archer: long tunic. **5, 6** Shield and spear. **7** Infantry soldier: short tunic, leather greaves. **8** Soldier: long tunic of leather plates. **9** Soldier: fringed shawl over armour. **10** Armed soldier: shawl around waist.

EUROPE 1 Lyre-player: long tunic, scarf at waist. **2** Serpent priestess: high tiara, tight-fitting bodice, skirt with apron. **3** Slave. **4** Noblewoman: elaborate hair-style. **5** Dancer: short-sleeved jacket over transparent bodice, layered skirt. **6** King: crown with lily design and feathers. **7** Noble: skirt with long tassel. **8** Noble: skirt with hanging belt. **9** Soldier: double apron, necklace-collar.

AFRICA 1 Child: shaven head, single long tuft of hair. **2** Slave. **3** Harp-player. **4** Slave playing drum. **5** Slave: long tunic with straps. **6** Noblewoman: garment knotted below bust, jewelled wig, precious collar. **7** High official: insignia of rank. **8** Pharaoh's standard-bearer. **9** Pharaoh: double crown, collar, decorated apron. **10** Queen: transparent robe over close-fitting tunic.

17TH CENTURY

PERSIA

RUSSIA

FRANCE

FRANCE

NORTH AMERICA

NORTH AMERICA

ASIA 1, 3 Servants. **2** Noble: belt with purse attached. **4** Pasha: large turban of various materials. **5** High-ranking officer: distinguishing shoulder-belt. **6** Merchant: coat with waist-sash, sleeves open on the inside. **7** Long waistcoat over tunic with small collar. **8** Gentleman: fancy coat with lapels, waist-sash. **9** Coat with open sleeves.

EUROPE 1 Coat over long waistcoat, shirt with long neck-cloth. **2** Button fastenings on back, sleeves and breeches. **3** Lace trimmings, wide lace collar. **4** Close-fitting gown, large pockets in skirt. **5** Plumed hat. **6, 7** Embroidered gloves and shoe. **8** Long buttoned coat, curled wig. **9** Walking clothes. **10** Wired linen and pleated lace fontange. **11, 12** Gentlewoman and child.

AMERICA 1 Deerskin cape with embroidery and shells (North Carolina). **2** Tattooed warrior. **3, 4** English colonists: armour, breeches, boots. **5** Buckskin skirt (Virginia). **6** Buckskin wrapped around the body and over one shoulder. **7** Warrior: scarifications and tattoos (Florida). **8, 9** Native American couple: buckskin clothing and moccasins.

17TH CENTURY INDIA JAPAN PERSIA

NETHERLANDS NETHERLANDS

Moors from Algeria and Morocco BENIN

ASIA 1 Prince: transparent muslin robe over trousers.
2 Sari, flowers in hair. **3** Sacrificial body-painting and
clothing. **4** Servant. **5** Noble: arrows in sash and
distinguishing hair-style. **6** Kimono. **7** Lady of the
court. **8** Retainer.

EUROPE 1, 2 Noblewoman and child. **3, 4** Burgher's
wife and child. **5** Burgher: lace-trimmed collar and cuffs.
6, 7 Lower-class woman and child. **8** Gentleman:
long coat, full breeches, bucket boots with spurs.
9 Gentlewoman: tight bodice, wide skirt on frame, ruff,
tall hat over lace bonnet. **10** Long gown, short overskirt.
11 Gentleman: high-waisted doublet, padded breeches.

AFRICA 1 Prince: military dress. **2** Prince: state dress.
3 Archer. **4** Warrior: hooded cloak. **5** Prince: scarification
on body, collar of beads and coral, skirt with Portuguese
heads. **6** Warrior: tall head-dress. **7** High-ranking warrior:
coral ornaments, lions' teeth, feather garment. **8** Warrior:
coral and cowrie-shell head-dress, collar and bangles.

CHINA

1000 BC

CHINA

SCANDINAVIA

SCANDINAVIA

Celts

Sarmatians

EGYPT

NUBIA

LIBYA

ASIA 1 Soldier: mail over tunic, carrying large shield.
2 Soldier: reinforced breastplate. **3** Soldier armed with
lance. **4** Official: wand of office. **5** Lady of the court: wide
kimono, hair-style indicating rank. **6** Hair-style of lady of
the court. **7** Helmet. **8** Slave. **9** Dignitary: cylindrical hat
fastened under the chin.

EUROPE 1 Stitched dress of woven wool. **2** Dress with
half-length sleeves, net bonnet. **3, 5** Warriors: short tunic
with shoulder-straps and buttons, cloak, fur hat. **4** Tunic,
short leather skirt. **6, 7, 8, 9** Bone comb, wool tassel,
brooch, fibula (Germano-Celtic). **10** Short belted tunic,
hat with turned-up brim (Hallstatt). **11** Horned helmet
(Hallstatt). **12** Archer: metal helmet, leather armour.

AFRICA 1 Princess: wig, perfumed cone, precious
necklace, transparent linen robe. **2** Spoons for ointments.
3 Box with writing materials. **4** Scribe. **5** Official:
leopard-skin sash. **6** Official: studded leather sash.
7, 8, 9 Dignitaries: tattooed body, cloak fastened over
one shoulder and at the waist, feather head-dress.

Phrygians   Parthians   **500 BC**   Parthians   Medes

Dacians   GREECE   GREECE

EGYPT   EGYPT   ECUADOR

ASIA 1 Tunic and trousers of embroidered leather, conical hat with top bent forward. **2** Princess: long embroidered garment. **3** Woman archer: embroidered leather. **4** Tunic fastened at the waist, wide trousers. **5** Mirror. **6, 7** Ornaments. **8** Archer: leather clothing. **9, 11** Servants. **10** Noble holding a mirror. **12** Bordered jacket, fastened with a belt, zouave trousers.

EUROPE 1 Archer: armour of leather plates. **2** Soldier: felt hat, long-sleeved tunic, cloak fastened at the neck. **3** Soldier: fringed cloak. **4** Huntress: peplos. **5** Long chiton. **6** Long chiton, cloak. **7** Short chiton with double belt. **8** Sandals. **9** Gold tiara. **10** Boots. **11** Long chiton, fastened over the arm to form sleeves.

AFRICA AND AMERICA 1 Dagger. **2** Mask representing the falcon-god Horus. **3** Coat of mail. **4** Bow. **5** High-ranking archer: characteristic head-dress. **6** Slave carrying flabellum. **7** Officer of archers. **8** Infantry soldier. **9, 10** Head-dresses. **11** Military standard. **12** Tabard of reinforced and decorated linen. **13** Male figurine: clothing painted on to the body (Chorrera).

16TH CENTURY   RUSSIA   INDIA   INDIA

ENGLAND   SPAIN   ENGLAND   FRANCE

Incas   *Incas*   *Inuit*

ASIA 1 Princess: tiara, long fur cloak embroidered on the outside. **2** Prince: diadem on head-dress, long sleeveless cloak embroidered on the outside. **3** Lady of the court. **4** Servant. **5** Archer: Mongolian dress. **6** Merchant: travelling dress. **7** Dignitary: long sash hanging in front. **8** Retainer.

EUROPE 1 Sleeveless fur-lined gown, cylindrical head-dress, veil under chin. **2** Tight-fitting sleeveless tunic, ruff, padded breeches. **3** Gentleman: high-collared cape. **4** Queen: high ruff, gown with wide skirt over frame. **5** Lady-in-waiting. **6** Page. **7** Servant: lace collar. **8** Queen: gown with wide skirt over frame, lace ruff. **9** Country dress of light material, open collar.

AMERICA 1 Dignitary: short wool tunic, geometric designs. **2** Noble: long striped tunic. **3** Double whistling jar. **4** Peasant. **5** Sealskin boot (Inuit). **6** Woman's anorak with hood. **7** Baby's suit of skin and fur (Inuit). **8, 9** Couple with baby: skins and furs with hoods. **10** Goggles. **11** Spear.

TURKEY   16TH CENTURY   TURKEY   RUSSIA

ENGLAND   ITALY   ITALY   GERMANY

Aztecs   *Aztecs*

ASIA 1 Noblewoman: indoor dress. **2** Market dress.
3 Veiled lady. **4** Sultan's guard. **5** Sultan: huge turban,
buttoned robe, small collar. **6** Officer of the guard.
7 Flag-bearer. **8** Mercenary: feather fixed in forehead,
heeled shoes. **9** Noble: fur-trimmed coat, tall fur hat.
10 Noble: fur-lined embroidered coat.

EUROPE 1 Noble: loose coat, fur collar. **2** King: padded
doublet, joined hose. **3** Lady of the court: bell-shaped
gown, puffed sleeves. **4** Venetian noble. **5** Gown with
padded shoulders, wide sleeves. **6** Wide-skirted gown,
puffed sleeves. **7** Noble: ruff, slashed tunic. **8** Queen:
bell-shaped gown. **9** Coat with puffed sleeves, side
pockets. **10** Mercenary: slashed doublet and breeches.

AMERICA 1 Priest: ceremonial dress. **2** Warrior chief:
nose and chin ornaments. **3** Warrior: body covered with
feathers, plumed head-dress. **4, 5** Warriors: jaguar skins,
feather ornaments, decorated shields. **6** Noble: tunic
decorated with feathers, tall head-dress, staff of office.

PERSIA   500 BC   CHINA

GREECE   GREECE

PERU   ECUADOR   PERU   ECU

ASIA 1 King: Median-style cloak, cylindrical hat.
2 Layered tunics, cloak with tassels, high conical turban.
3 King: long cloak. **4** High-ranking soldier: tunic, trousers of embroidered leather. **5** Soldier: leather mail. **6** Servant: kimono over fitting trousers. **7** Saddle of embroidered leather (Siberia). **8** Archer. **9** Retainer. **10** Soldier with lance.

EUROPE 1, 2 Robes draped over one shoulder, as worn by philosophers and orators. **3** Flute-player. **4** Pleated tunic, fastened below waist and hanging from shoulders. **5** Coloured fabric, open at one side and fastened at waist. **6** Child: draped robe. **7** Travelling costume, wide-brimmed hat. **8, 9** Hoplites: leather and metal armour, crested helmets. **10** Soldier: breastplate, metal helmet.

AMERICA 1 Tunic, woven fabric with gold leaf (Nazca). **2** Sandals with turquoise studs (Moche). **3** Gold crown (Moche). **4** Noble: long tunic, quilted head-dress. **5** Warrior: quilted tunic and helmet. **6** Priest (Moche). **7** Painted body (Manteño). **8** Noble (Bahia). **9** Woven fabric (Paracas). **10** Gold and turquoise earrings (Moche). **11** Necklaces, earrings, feathered head-dress (Bahia).

INDIA AFGHANISTAN **1ST CENTURY AD** PERSIA

Etruscans ROME ROME

ETHIOPIA CARTHAGE

ASIA 1 Noble: kimono jacket, long tunic. **2, 3** Princes: precious necklaces, turbans. **4** Queen: crown, long tunic sewn with precious stones (Kushan). **5** Noble warrior: clothes sewn with gold and precious stones (Kushan). **6, 7, 8** Princesses: clothes and head-dresses sewn with precious stones (Kushan). **9, 10, 11** King's head-dresses. **12** Noble: crown, tunic knotted at waist.

EUROPE 1 Flute-player: cloak wrapped around body. **2** Flute-player: long-sleeved embroidered tunic, shawl, conical cap. **3, 4** Legionaries: helmets, metal and leather armour. **5** Public official: toga with border to indicate rank. **6** Lictor. **7, 8** Plebeian woman and child. **9** Farmer: short tunic, wide-brimmed hat. **10** Centurion: armour, helmet trimmed with horsehair.

AFRICA 1 Dignitary: hanging studded sash, feathers in cap. **2** Notable: full tunic, decorated cloak. **3** Dignitary. **4, 5** Queen and king, the former with fringed sash. **6** Priest's assistant: white tunic, belt at waist. **7** Slave: skirt, apron. **8** Noblewoman: flat-topped head-dress, robe with geometric designs. **9** Priestess: crown, collar, winged skirt over long tunic.

15TH CENTURY

INDIA   INDIA   TURKEY

GERMANY   FRANCE   FRANCE   ENGLAND

Incas   *Incas*

ASIA 1 Servant: muslin dress over trousers, head-veil.
2, 3 Princes: silk robes, turbans. **4, 5** Snake-charmer.
6 Moslem merchant. **7** Servant: material draped to form
wide trousers. **8** Merchant: shawl over one shoulder,
fastened at waist with a belt. **9** Pasha: tall turban, open
caftan over long robe. **10** Soldier: horsehair head-dress
with wings of bird of prey.

EUROPE 1 Official: coat-sleeves slashed at elbow.
2, 3 Short doublets, sleeves open in front. **4** Fur-lined
cloak, sleeves open behind. **5** Cloak, sleeves open at the
side. **6** Heart-shaped head-dress, low-cut gown, full
undergown. **7** Waisted doublet, pointed soled hose.
8 Pointed head-dress with veil. **9** Over-doublet open at
the sides. **10** Square neck, long bodice, bell-shaped skirt.

AMERICA 1 Tunic, embroidered sash. **2** Child: knee-
length tunic. **3** Poncho (Titicaca). **4, 9, 10** Nose
ornaments (Milagro-Quevedo). **5** Noble: tunic, tall head-
dress. **6** Noble: knee-length skirt. **7** Noble: scarf knotted
over tunic, tall head-dress indicating rank. **8** Noble:
ceremonial dress. **11** Priest: ceremonial dress, sun-disc.
12 Noble girl: ceremonial dress, white veil.

ITALY   NETHERLANDS

Aztecs   *Aztecs*

ASIA 1 Temple guardian. **2, 3** Gold appliqués. **4** Nobelwoman: long fur cloak. **5, 6** Nobles: fur cloaks embroidered on the outside, frog fastenings. **7** Gentleman. **8** Lady: long surcoat over petticoat with apron. **9** Official: distinguishing sash, pointed slippers. **10** Village headman: light tunic over trousers.

EUROPE 1 Coat, open bag sleeves. **2** Sleeveless fur-trimmed tunic. **3** Long trailing sleeves, padded roll head-dress. **4, 5** Nobles: doublets, sleeveless coats, particoloured hose. **6** Banker: tall broad-brimmed hat, fur-trimmed gown. **7** Rich bourgoise: dress raised to reveal underskirt. **8** Padded roll head-dress with lace. **9** Heart-shaped head-dress. **10** Horned head-dress, draped veil.

AMERICA 1 Noble: cloak knotted over one shoulder, open at the side. **2** Warrior: spectacular feather head-dress. **3** Long-sleeved shirt. **4** Noble with fan. **5** Sleeveless shirt, calf-length skirt. **6** Hunter: wild-cat skin on head and shoulders. **7** Tunic, skirt. **8, 9** Priests: ceremonial dress.

PERSIA BYZANTIUM **5TH CENTURY** CHINA

ROME *Celts* *Gallo-Romans* *Germans*

Mayas NORT

ASIA 1 Prince: crown, tunic sewn with pearls and jewels over long, puffed trousers, shoes with ribbons. **2, 3** Princes. **4** Imperial guard: necklace, shield with chi-rho monogram. **5** Official: full cloak over knee-length tunic. **6, 7** Emperor and empress: crowns, tunics, jewelled shoes. **8** Pan-pipe-player. **9** Drummer.

EUROPE 1 Emperor as a soldier. **2** Emperor: toga, laurel crown. **3** Praetorian guard. **4** Warrior: conical hat, tunic, trousers. **5** Farmer: Woven fabric and leather. **6** Embroidered tunic with notched edge, striped shawl. **7** Hooded cloak. **8** Helmet. **9** Brooch and neck-ring. **10** Dress with halter-neck, belted at the waist. **11** Warrior: long tunic, helmet with wild-boar emblem.

AMERICA 1 Dignitary: full cloak, tall head-dress with feathers. **2** Priest: distinguishing head-dress. **3** Tunic with geometric design. **4, 5** Tattooed warriors. **6, 7** Priests: ceremonial dress, head-dresses and jaguar skins to indicate status. **8** King: feather head-dress and shield, jade ornaments (Freemont).

Franks   *Franks*   FRANCE

AMERICA   *Mayas*   *Mayas*

ASIA 1 Cavalry soldier: head-dress, long tunic of reinforced leather. **2, 3** Tochari couple: embroidered tunics with geometric designs. **4, 5** Emperor and empress: ceremonial dress, the head-dresses and fullness of sleeves showing their status. **6** Princess. **7, 8** Servants. **9** High official: distinguishing hat with ribbon.

EUROPE 1 Warrior: leather trousers, hair tied in pony-tail. **2, 3** Warriors: various types of armour, helmets, shields. **4** King: tunic, short cloak. **5** Queen: layered tunics, short cape around the shoulders. **6, 7** Royal crowns. **8, 9** Shoes. **10** Member of the imperial guard. **11** Noblewoman: cloak covering the head, fastened with two brooches. **12** Imperial official: staff of office.

AMERICA 1, 2 Warriors: painted bodies (Mimbres). **3** Priest: staff to indicate status, skull painted on face. **4** Priest: jaguar head and skin to indicate status. **5** Jar with screw lid (Guatemala). **6** Warrior: crocodile head-dress. **7** Warrior: hair in pony-tail, worn forward. **8** Noble: head-dress representing a wild cat.

1   2   3   4   5   6   7   8   9

ENGLAND   ENGLAND   FRANCE

1   2   3   4   5   6   7   8   9   10

NIGERIA   *Incas*   *Aztecs*

1   2   3   4   5   6

ASIA 1 Soldier: helmet, leather greaves. **2** King. **3** Slave. **4, 5** Princesses: richly decorated clothing, head-veils. **6** Prince: draped dhoti forming wide trousers. **7** Temple guardian. **8** Princess: collar and epaulettes over bare breasts. **9** Dancer: pagoda head-dress.

EUROPE 1 Courtier: roll head-dress, pointed boots. **2** Jester. **3** Peasant woman: apron. **4** Peasant: hat worn over hood. **5** Woodcutter. **6, 7** King and queen: ermine capes. **8** Lady of the court: low-necked dress, garland of flowers. **9** Lady of the court: square-necked surcoat, roll head-dress. **10** Lady of the court: buttoned dress, braided hair.

AFRICA AND AMERICA 1, 2 Faces with scarification and necks elongated with rings (Ife). **3** King: regal parasol and staff of office, feather head-dress. **4** King: elaborately patterned and coloured tunic. **5** King: cloak knotted across the chest. **6** Priest: ceremonial dress with large pectoral-apron, feather head-dress, long cloak.

ITALY

ITALY

SPAIN

NIGERIA

MALI

BENIN

ASIA 1 Servant: lynx-fur bonnet. **2** Infantry soldier: leather and chain-mail armour. **3** Archer: long leather tunic. **4** Servant: fur hat. **5** Metal helmet inlaid with silver. **6** King: fur cloak, embroidered leather tunic. **7** Cavalry soldier. **8** Dignitary: fur cloak, embroidered at the shoulders. **9** High official: elaborate helmet, jacket knotted across the chest, armour.

EUROPE 1 Knight: fur-lined cloak. **2** Noble. **3** Hooded cap, as worn by the guild of doctors. **4** Doctor. **5** Noble: 'page-boy' haircut. **6** Doge: ermine cape. **7** Bishop. **8** Noblewoman: horned head-dress, fur cape, full sleeves. **9** Lady of the court.

AFRICA 1 Warrior: tunic of reinforced leather. **2** Serpent goddess (Jenne-Jeno). **3** Warrior figure: elaborate disc head-dress (Tada). **4** Servant (Tada). **5** High-ranking dignitary: disc head-dress, shell and leopard's teeth necklace (Tada). **6** King: crown, coral necklace, bracelets and ankle-rings (Ife). **7** Court dwarf. **8, 9** Tattooed warriors: quilted leather and fabric headwear.

BYZANTIUM   12TH CENTURY   ARABIA

1   2   3   4   5   6   7   8   9   10   11

FRANCE   *Normans*   *Anglo- Normans*   GERMANY

1   2   3   4   5   6   7   8   9

Mayas   *Mayas*

1   2   3   4   5   6   7

ASIA 1 Princess: sleeveless tunic, long undergarment.
2 Empress: wide collar, long jewelled sash. **3** Emperor:
military dress. **4, 5, 6, 7** Imperial crown, collar, shoe,
glove. **8** Merchant. **9** Archer. **10** Infantry soldier.
11 Cavalry soldier.

EUROPE 1 Priest. **2** Commoner: hood, bound hose.
3, 4, 5 Soldiers: various types of armour. **6** King: military
dress, shield with coat-of-arms, closed helmet. **7** Bishop.
8 Knight's squire. **9** Princess: crown, veil fastened below
the chin, snood for the hair.

AMERICA 1 Noble: distinguishing head-dress, staff
of office. **2** Priest: skirt decorated with jaguar skin.
3 Priest's assistant. **4, 5** Noblewoman and child.
6 Important dignitary: staff of office. **7** Warrior: obsidian
sword.

ENGLAND   ENGLAND

MEXICO   MEXICO   COLOMBIA

ASIA 1 Dignitary: long caftan buttoned over tunic with small collar. **2** Peasant woman: shawl around head. **3** Fur cloak, fur-trimmed hat. **4** Child: coat with frog fastenings. **5, 6** Ceremonial head-dress and sword. **7** Prince in state dress. **8** Schoolmaster. **9, 10** Buddhist monks with shaven heads.

EUROPE 1 Belted long tunic, hair net. **2** Doctor: distinguishing head-dress. **3** Child: summer clothing. **4** Servant. **5** Child: winter clothing. **6** Architect: beret, hood. **7** Hunter: long tunic, zouave trousers. **8** Shepherd: hood, shoulder-cape. **9** Crown. **10** Belt with purse for alms. **11** Brooch. **12** Shoes of different styles. **13** Knight: full armour. **14** Knight: cloak over armour.

AMERICA 1 Dignitary (Aztec). **2** King on jaguar throne (Aztec). **3** Noble (Aztec). **4** Warrior (Aztec). **5** Priest: ceremonial dress, distinguishing jaguar skin (Aztec). **6, 7** Pendants for necklaces. **8** Figurine: sash tied around waist. **9** Pin with bird figure. **10** Pin with human figure. **11, 13** Component parts of earrings. **12** Necklace bead in form of a human head.

ENGLAND FRANCE ITALY

PERU PERU

ASIA 1 Princess: elaborate head-dress, long scarf wrapped around body to indicate status. **2** Lady of the court. **3** Beggar. **4** Queen: full-sleeved tunic to indicate status. **5, 6** Officials: distinguishing head-dress and batons of rank. **7** Full armour and helmet. **8** Archer: long leather armour.

EUROPE 1 King: sleeveless tunic over undergarment. **2** Queen: long-sleeved gown, long cloak. **3** Peasant: bonnet. **4** Bird-seller. **5** Noble: cloak split at the sides, full sleeves, hat with turned-up brim. **6** Noblewoman: layered tunics of different lengths, cloak. **7** Knee-length overgarment. **8** Hood with extended point (liripipe), pointed shoes.

AMERICA 1 Gold crown (Chimù). **2** Metal ornament for sewing on to fabric. **3** Sacrificial knife. **4** Anthropomorphic tweezers. **5** Tiara. **6** Plume. **7** Dignitary (Chimù). **8** King: feathered head-dress, (Chimù). **9** Noble: mace, distinguishing head-dress. **10** Noblewoman: dress with precious decoration to indicate status. **11** Noble: short layered tunics.